CW00407310

A BOOT UP

NORTH CORNWALL'S SITES OF MAGIC AND MYSTERY

Terry Faull

First published in Great Britain in 2010

Photography copyright © 2010 David Spires, text copyright © 2010 Terry Faull

Front cover: *Path to Bossiney Haven* © Terry Faull

British Library Cataloguing-in-Publication Data
A CIP record for this title is available from the British Library

ISBN 978 1 906887 93 3

PiXZ Books
Halsgrove House, Ryelands Industrial Estate,
Bagley Road, Wellington, Somerset TA21 9PZ
Tel: 01823 653777
Fax: 01823 216796
email: sales@halsgrove.com

An imprint of Halstar Ltd, part of the Halsgrove group of companies
Information on all Halsgrove titles is available at: www.halsgrove.com

Printed and bound in China by Toppan Leefung Printing Ltd

Contents

North Cornwall's Sites of Magic and Mystery

Introduction

The far north of Cornwall is a remote district of deep wooded valleys, secret paths and ancient churches. Its history is full of strange characters, family rivalries, hauntings, smuggling and forgotten mysteries. The Atlantic Ocean is on one side, to the south lies Bodmin Moor with Exmoor and Dartmoor looming on the horizon to the north and east. This is frontier land. The River Tamar rises here and is the county boundary with Devon and it once separated the Anglo-Saxons of Wessex from the Celts of Cornwall.

The land hungry Anglo-Saxons pushed across the Tamar and the *ton*, *cott* and *worthy* place names show where they settled. From Poundstock southwards, the old Cornish words *tre*, *pol* and *pen* mark farms and villages where the native Celts held on the longest.

This area is rich in stories and legends. The ten walks in this book explore places where there are such stories to be told and where magic and mystery can still be found.

The Walks

None of these walks is more than five miles long and all are intended for those who enjoy a leisurely amble of discovery. The routes follow public rights of way or land open for access. In a few cases short stretches of roadway are included. These lanes are narrow and sometimes carry farm traffic or speeding motorists, so please take care.

There is a sketch map at the start of each walk and information about the terrain to be covered together with grid references to help you locate the starting point on Ordnance Survey maps Explorer 111 & 126.

Several of the routes follow tree-lined valleys which have been cut into the inland plateau by fast flowing streams running to reach the sea. These coombes shelter ancient farms, churches and hidden paths which take you to the cliffs and link up with the South West Coast Path.

Coast view

Poundstock church

Key to Symbols Used

Level of difficulty:

Easy 🍂

Moderate 🍂 🍂

More Challenging 🍂 🍂 🍂

Map symbols:

🚗	Park & start
⎯⎯⎯	Tarred Road
- - -	Footpath
▬ ▬ ▬	Walk Footpath
■	Building
+	Church
▲	Triangulation pillar or other landmark
🚻	WC
🍴	Refreshments
🍺	Pub

Walk Locations

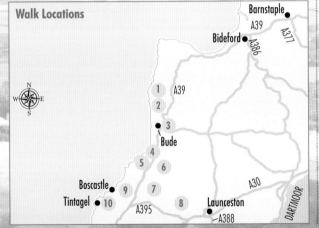

Barnstaple
A39
A377
Bideford
A386

1 A39
2
3
Bude
4
5   6
9   7
Boscastle
Tintagel 10   8
A395   Launceston
A388
A30
DARTMOOR

N W E S

Morwenstow and Tonacombe

Two haunted manors, a double tragedy and a wreckers coast.

Level: 🥾🥾
Length: 2.5 miles
Terrain: Some steep sections and coast path walking
Parking: By Morwenstow church
Start Ref: SS 205153
Explorer Map 126

Morwenstow has always been rather remote; this isolation is reflected in the strange characters and events reported from here. This walk starts at the church where an eccentric Victorian rector ministered to his flock, it passes two ancient manor houses before reaching the dramatic coast. Many sailing ships were driven on to the rocks here sometimes lured by false lanterns. The final section is along a special valley, home to a rare butterfly.

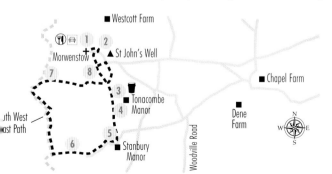

Track to Tonacombe

1. There is car parking near the church. Perched on the side of a valley overlooking the sea, there are few churches with a more romantic setting. It has a magnificent Norman doorway, an ancient font and a frieze of mythical animal heads on some interior arches. Robert Stephen Hawker who was the rector here from 1834 to 1875, would sometimes come to church wearing a flowing white cloak, accompanied by a pet pig. Dressed in a knitted fisherman's jersey and long sea boots, Hawker was often the first to reach the nearby cliffs when there was a shipwreck; he buried many drowned seafarers in Morwenstow churchyard.

2. From the church, return through the lychgate to the nearby drive to the rectory; just before the rectory gate, follow the National Trust sign to St John's Holy Well. The attractive little well house is in a corner of the rectory garden; water from it is used for baptisms just as it has been for hundreds of years.

View at Morwenstow

The first modern Harvest Festival service was held in Morwenstow church to give thanks for a good harvest in 1842.

Morwenstow church

3 From the well, cross over the green in front of the Rectory Farm tearooms and follow the yellow waymark through the farmyard gate and across the field to the stile in the far hedge. Turn left up the lane and through the gate to Crosstown and then through the beer garden in front of the Bush Inn. Continue down the sloping field to the left hand corner where a kissing gate leads into a wooded area. At the bottom of the steps, ignore the sign pointing to the coast path and continue straight ahead over the slate bridge. Follow the cobbled pathway up a narrow track and out into a field; keep to the left then across the middle of the next field towards Tonacombe Manor.

4 Take the path between stone hedges straight ahead to reach a track. On the left there is a splendid gateway into the yard of what has been described as the perfect Tudor manor; it is also haunted. One apparition is of a short man dressed in black; another is of a lady dressed in Elizabethan clothing and carrying a bunch of keys. The sound of something being dragged across the floor has also been heard. The walk goes through the fieldgate on the right of the Manor gateway, across the middle of the next two fields to a stone stile and on to the farm road at Stanbury Manor.

5 The Manor (behind the farm buildings) like its close neighbour, is haunted. Here the ghostly feature is an ancient chest containing an evil presence. The legend tells how two old women, were struck deaf by the evil spirits released when they opened the box. The chest was banished to Stanbury with a curse of bad luck if it was ever moved again. In the 16th century Stanbury Manor was owned by John Manning who fell in love with Christiana the daughter of the vicar of Morwenstow. They married but shortly afterwards John was gored to death by a bull. Tragically, on finding his body, Christiana miscarried her baby and also died. The Manor then passed to 5 aunts — perhaps it was two of these ladies who went deaf when they opened the haunted chest.

6 Turn down the farm track towards the coast. Continue past the first car parking area and at a

The giant aerials across the valley from Stanbury are part of an international electronic monitoring network.

second grassy area, walk along the track straight ahead. This soon enters a field where you follow the fenced off path to reach the cliff. The jagged rocks of this a dramatic coastline stretch out from the shore and it is easy to imagine how sailing ships came to grief on these reefs. Shipwrecked cargoes represented unaccustomed riches to local people who lived in this wild area. There are secret paths down to the shore which were once used by smugglers and other local people who came to see what harvest the storms had brought.

7 Follow the coast path along to the right and then down the steep valley side to a little steam at Tidna Shute. Leave the coastpath here and turn inland along the bottom of the valley. Wind-bent trees are

evidence of the extreme weather conditions along this coast and it is remarkable that this was one of the last strongholds for the delicate large blue butterfly. The large blue has a remarkable life cycle. It lays its eggs only on wild thyme plants and as the larvae feed, they leave a sugary secretion. This attracts red ants who take the larvae down into their nests where they overwinter to emerge the following summer as fully grown butterflies. Traditional farming practices and wild rabbits ensured that thyme and colonies of red ants could flourish here and so the large blue survived after it had vanished elsewhere in Britain.

Stile at Stanbury

Soay sheep on cliff path

(8) Continue along the path to the waymark sign pointing up hill, this path returns you to the lane leading to Crosstown and so back to the car park.

2 **Coombe and Stowe**

The first Cornish mole and the lost Great House of Stowe.

Coombe Valley has everything needed for a Cornish seaside holiday – a cove, old cottages and farms, village amenities at Kilkhampton and a network of footpaths. This walk passes through some of the places associated with mysterious events and stories from its history.

Level: 🐾🐾
Length: 3.5 miles
Terrain: Level paths and two steep sections
Parking: In lay-by next to gate to Coombe.
Start Ref: SS 208116
Explorer Map 126

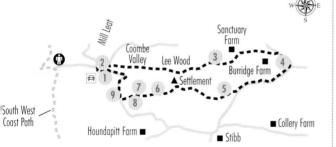

South West Coast Path

Mill Leat
Coombe Valley
Lee Wood
Sanctuary Farm
Burridge Farm
Settlement
Houndapitt Farm
Stibb
Collery Farm

Stream at Ford

Coombe Mill

1 Leave your car in the lay-by beside the road at Coombe (on the road near the turning down to the coast at Duckpool) and go through the gate and across the footbridge towards the watermill. There has been a mill here for over 300 years and this like the other properties in Coombe, is owned by the Landmark Trust. Walk past the restored water wheel to the cob and thatch cottage beside the stream.

2 The cottage by the ford was home to a beautiful dark haired girl called Alice. This blue eyed beauty was courted by suitors for miles around but she had set her heart on marrying the young Grenville, heir to nearby Stowe House. A ball was planned at Stowe and Alice bought a gown of darkest velvet and

Ford Cottage

Part of Chapel Cottage, one of the holiday homes at Coombe. In 1860 there existed here a chapel on wheels which could be moved around to places where there was a congregation who lacked a building to hold services.

3 From Ford Cottage take the narrow path which goes behind the millhouse and along Coombe Valley. Continue out into the forestry following the track until it starts to swing to the right down towards the stream, continue along the narrow path straight ahead and out into a field. Keep to the left hand hedge and join the narrow farm track to Sanctuary Farm. Walk past the converted

persuaded her widowed mother to let her wear the family heirloom, a fine silver ring. Alice admired herself in the mirror and whispered *"If Grenville is not to be mine, then all prayers are a waste of time"*. With these words Alice vanished and was never seen again.

Some months afterwards, a gardener at Tonacombe Manor saw a silver ring poking out of a mound of newly turned earth. On hearing a faint cry, he saw a small blind creature with a dark velvet coat, crawling along the ground — the first mole ever seen in Cornwall!

Flowers along the forestry track

buildings and out along the access drive until you reach the public road. Turn right downhill.

4 At the crossroads, take the narrow road on the right. This is the heart of the Valley; inland you can glimpse Kilkhampton on the ancient ridgeway once used by travellers who wished to avoid the sea journey along the treacherous North Cornish coast.

5 Walk along the narrow road which gradually rises up the Valley side. Continue until you reach a lane on the right hand side; this is the old carriage road to Stowe and called "Iron" or "High Horn" Hill where the coachman would sound his horn to alert the servants at the House that members of the Grenville family were coming. Follow this lane, then along the top of a field and into the woodland beyond. A number of tracks lead through

the trees and you should choose one which leads down into the Valley forestry plantation. Close to the bottom on the right is the site of an Iron Age hill fort; where the forestry track divides, turn left (rather than right and over the concrete bridge which joins the outward route) and follow the track uphill.

6 After a short walk, the track narrows and then reaches a field gate. Straight ahead is the route

17th century wall

of the old carriage drive to Stowe. Follow this past a brick wall on the right which dates from 1675 and was one of the enclosures which surrounded Stowe House.

7 The wall leads to a long low building. In recent times it has been used to house cattle, however it is a mystery. Some sources say it is the remains of a real tennis court, the game favoured by the ladies and gentleman of the royal court following the restoration of the monarchy in 1660. If it is such a remnant, then it is a rare survivor. The grassy terraces and hollows in the field to the left are all that remain of the Great House of Stowe. This was built in grand style by John Grenville. Stowe was the height of fashion with assembly rooms

Real Tennis Court?

and parlours decorated with fine carvings, a private chapel and fine formal gardens.

8 However Stowe was a doomed manor. When John Grenville died in 1701, as his son, Charles, journeyed home for the funeral, he was killed in an accident while cleaning a pistol. The next heir was 7 year old William Henry who only lived 10 more years before dying of

smallpox. Ownership of the estate was the subject of a prolonged family dispute and eventually in1720, Stowe came to Grace one of John's daughters who seldom visited Stowe and it gradually fell into disuse. In 1739 the house was dismantled and the fittings and building materials sold off. Bits of Stowe were taken away to become part of several other West Country houses and the new town Hall at South Molton. All that remained at

Stowe were the former servants' and domestic quarters which became the present farm house. The site of Stowe and its gardens became overgrown.

(9) Cross diagonally over the field in front of the farm house and out through the gate on to the road. Stowe has one further surprise; next to the road and in front of the curtain-wall there is a narrow gully. This is the carriage wash – a kind of very early carwash – where carriages would be washed off before the Grenvilles and their guests travelled out. From here it is a short walk downhill to Coombe; this is along the road so do take care (alternatively go back along the path and down into the forestry plantation from where you can make your way back along the route from Coombe).

Stowe

Old carriage wash

3 **Launcells and Stratton**

A holy well, King Alfred's Will, William Morris and a real giant.

St Swithin's church at Launcells was described by John Betjeman as "the least spoiled church in Cornwall". It boasts a Tudor wall painting, Georgian box pews and early patterned floor tiles. The walk from here is along green lanes and across river bridges to reach Stratton, the home of a true giant.

Level: 🥾🥾
Length: 2.75 miles
Terrain: Fields and lanes with one steep section.
Parking: At Launcells church
Start Ref: SS 244057
Explorer Map 111

St Swithin's holy well

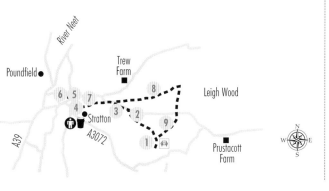

There is parking at Launcells church. Before exploring this special building, visit the Holy Well tucked in below the roadbridge (try not to visit on 15 July because if it rains, there will be 40 more wet days to come). Inside, the church is full of light from the clear glass windows; there are ancient bench ends and splendid 15th century encaustic floor tiles with patterns of gothic beasts and flowers, in the chancel. Near the door, there are the remains of a wall painting depicting the sacrifice of Isaac, a reminder that many country church interiors were once enlivened by brightly-coloured paintings.

From here, follow the path out through the gate in the top left of the churchyard, cross the drive into a narrow lane. At the top of this path,

Launcells church

15th century floor tiles

turn left and go into the field ahead via the kissing gate. Keeping to the left hand side, walk down hill and through another field until you reach the wooded area ahead. Follow the path into the trees and over the bridge across the stream and then make your way up a narrow lane to the road; turn left here.

(3) Walk along the road. Look out for a little slate plaque in the hedge-bottom where Smallridge Lane joins this road; this marks the boundary between the old Stratton Urban and Rural Districts. (Remember this as you will need to take Smallridge Lane on the return leg of this walk). Continue along the road to reach the hamlet of Diddies where just before the bridge, you join a footpath on the left through the gate marked Trevennen.

Sir Goldsworthy Gurney, who is buried in Launcells churchyard, was a noted Victorian inventor who developed the special navigation light used in lighthouses, a central heating system for warming large buildings such as cathedrals and a floating concrete raft system for building on sand.

(4) The route now crosses and re-crosses a stream by a series of footbridges. Continue along until you reach the car park at Stratton (on the way look out for an arched garden gate made out of a pile of logs and providing a home for wildlife). Stratton was the administrative centre of a Saxon Hundred and is mentioned in the 9th century will of King Alfred leaving this land to his eldest son. There is much to explore in this pretty little township.

Slate boundary marker

5 From the car park, turn right by the thatched cottage, along Spicers Lane and up the hill towards the church. Just before the top of this lane, look out for a cobbled path on the left and turn into this to reach Gibraltar Square; This is dominated by a fine house with plaques of 1785 and marking the 17th Regiment of Foot. These commemorate Robert Smith who retired here after being wounded at

Log pile gate

the Siege of Gibraltar. Go through the little narrow archway in the left hand corner of the Square and along the Drangway to reach the green and war memorial in front of the church.

6 Turn left, down hill, past the old bank building on the right and left at the road junction. A few yards on the right is the entrance to the Tree Inn. In 1643 it was the headquarters of the Royalist army before the Battle of Stamford Hill which was fought nearby. On the wall inside the courtyard of the inn, there is a full size painting of Anthony Payne, who fought at Stamford Hill and who lived here. Anthony was 7ft. 4ins. tall, with tremendous strength and a quick mind; after the Restoration of the monarchy he became a favourite of

King Charles. After Anthony died, his body was too big to bring down the stairs and so a hatchway had to be cut in the floor and the coffin was lowered down (the hatchway can still be seen in the Inn).

Anthony Payne

Walking across the stream

From the Tree Inn, return to the church. In marked contrast to St Swithin's, here the windows are mostly stained glass. The east window is of particular note having been designed by Burne-Jones and William Morris. The church holds relics from the Battle of Stamford Hill and also has a fine memorial brass from the 16th century. There has been a church here since Saxon times but the present building which dates mostly from the 14th and 15th centuries and was heavily restored in 1888. Leave the churchyard by the little gate in the top right hand wall and walk down Sanctuary Lane, then cross over the road at the bottom towards Drovers Way. Walk down here and a few yards along on the right you will find a narrow footpath. This will take you back to the river where you should turn left to return to Diddies and the slate boundary marker at Smallridge Lane.

The route is now up this Lane; a steady climb. Near the top and where the lane begins to turn into a narrow farm track, look across the valley on the left towards the signs of earthworks in a field. This is East Leigh Berrys where the Normans carried out preparatory work for a motte and bailey fortified site but never completed building; perhaps things had become more peaceful and

Back to Launcells

a stronghold was no longer needed. From here the tracks gets narrower and sometimes muddy but continue along until the junction with another lane, where you should turn right.

(9) Follow the lane downhill (take care as the surface is badly rutted in places) then up again until it reaches a road at Cross Lanes. Cross straight over the road and into the field where a signpost helpfully says 650 metres to Launcells church. The footpath goes across to the top right hand corner of this field, over a stile, then across the centre of the next two fields to reach the far right hand corner where it meets the path and the kissing gate you went through earlier. Retrace your steps to the church.

4 Poundstock, Millook and Trebarfoote

*A murdered priest, a rediscovered saint, smugglers
and a haunted house.*

From the church and its unique gildhouse, this walk goes to the coast to find ancient rocks in a smugglers' cove and then back inland through a valley with protected woodlands and past a manor house with a ghost and a romantic and tragic history.

Level: 🥾 🥾
Length: 2.5 miles
Terrain: Fields and lanes with one steep section
Parking: In the car park close to Poundstock church
Start Ref: SX 203995
Explorer Map 111

Cliffs at Millook

1 A new car park has been provided above the church just a short walk downhill into the churchyard. Ahead are the church and the historic gildhouse which is the only one of its kind to survive in Cornwall. This remote spot has a turbulent history including the murder of a priest, William Penfound, in 1357. At that time the area was ravaged by a gang of smugglers led by members of the local landowning families. There was a quarrel within the ranks of these ruffians and the Penfound family fell out with the main gang. In revenge, a group of men forced their way into the church attacking members of the family including William who was hacked to death in front of his altar.

2 The church has seen some amusing events, including an incident in 1535 when two irate husbands hammered on the vicarage door while the curate helped his current mistress escape over the back wall! It has also rediscovered its true name; after the Reformation, the protestant church leaders destroyed all references to the patron saint of Poundstock. Later it was believed that the dedication had been to St Neot but research in the 1940s showed that the original patron saint at Poundstock was the 6th century St Winwalloe.

3 In the 15th century the church was rebuilt and extended and the gildhouse was built. Over time this became the centre of social life for the parish including the church ales or feasts which could sometimes last for days. In the 19th century it was the local poorhouse, then a day school, parish library and meeting room. It fell in disuse but has now been rescued and restored; during this work a sealed glass bottle was found behind the great fireplace. This may contain a charm as it was once common practice to hide such items as protection against evil spirits.

A house on the main road near Poundstock church was once a public house called the Turk's Head and may have taken its name from the figurehead of a ship used by smugglers; it lost its licence in 1903.

Gildhouse

(4) From the church take the road to Trevissick and follow this until, just before the farm, a track branches to the left; this leads to a field gate ahead. Go through the gate and across the middle of the field, as you go over the brow of the hill, head towards the woodland in the right hand corner. Here you will find a track which leads over a footbridge and through the woodland until it reaches an open area next to a cottage. Walk through this and over the stream and then turn right until you reach the road down to the shore at Millook.

(5) The zigzag rocks in the cliffs here were formed some 320 million years ago and are amongst the finest examples of such geological formations in Britain. Millook was a notorious centre for smugglers and wreckers. When a cargo of 500 barrels of spirits was landed here in 1820, the customs men pounced but were soon beaten off by the smugglers. This cargo would have been transported on pack horses inland and the walk now follows an old smuggler's path up the Millook Valley. From the beach return to the footbridge near the cottage and with the stream on your left, continue along the track straight ahead.

Gildhouse entrance

6 The steep hillsides are covered in dense deciduous woodland, of special scientific interest because of its wild creatures and plants. Shortly after going through a gate look out for a path on the left which takes you over the stream and up into more woods. The path winds around the hill and eventually out into a field where you should follow the way along the left hand hedge and towards the buildings of Trebarfoote

Manor. On reaching the Manor, a track will lead you past some buildings; with the main house on your left; follow the drive out but pause to look back through the ornamental iron gates at Trebarfoote.

7 This ancient house has a long history. It was used by smugglers, suffered attack during the Civil War and had a ballroom which was used for dancing and wild parties in the 1920s. Most interesting of all is

Trebarfoote Manor

the story of the two lovers who were shot while eloping and the ghost which has haunted the Manor ever since. Some 400 years ago, there was a feud between the squire who lived in Trebarfoote and his neighbour at nearby Penfound Manor. However his daughter and the young heir to Penfound fell in love and when they were forbidden to marry, they decided to elope only to be discovered. During the argument which followed, both the young lovers were killed and ever since then there has been a tradition that her ghost haunts Trebarfoote. In the 1970s the new owners of Trebarfoote traced a smell of perfume to a long disused attic room and under the floorboards; they found a miniature painting of a young woman in 17th century dress. Since then there have not been any sightings of a ghost.

(8) Follow the drive away from Trebarfoote and continue along the road to the junction where you turn down left to Poundstock church.

Millook Valley

5 Dizzard

A mermaid, a stunted wood and a smugglers' path.

A trail which winds along the coast past an ancient woodland of natural bonsai trees which is a scheduled site of special site of scientific interest, then inland to a trail once used by brandy smugglers.

Level:
Length: 3.6 miles
Terrain: Fields and woods with steep sections
Parking: Small lay-by at Cancleave
Start Ref: SX 176993
Explorer Map 111

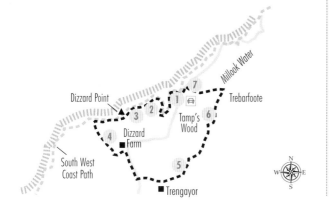

Dizzard Wood

On the switchback road from Millook towards Dizzard you will find a small lay-by on the inland side of the road near Cancleave. From here follow the footpath sign towards the sea to join the coast path. Turn left and down into a wooded valley then across a small stream and up again out into a field. From here there are splendid views up the coast and beyond.

Continue along the coast path. On the seaward side, the cliffs fall away down to the rocky shoreline at Sharnhole Point; it was near here that a mermaid was seen swimming along and singing sweetly. She was spied twice sitting on a rock twisting her golden hair; an old man told me this tale of his youth and assured me it was true. He described how he tried to catch hold of the beauty but she slipped from his grasp into the sea and re-surfaced some yards away "grinning just like a seal!"

Soon after the next field hedge you will reach Dizzard Point where a surveyor's pillar leans seawards, an indication that the land here is slowly slipping. A series of landslips are clothed in ancient woodland. The trees have been stunted by the onshore salt winds and in places you can stand like a Gulliver with an ancient forest at waist height growing all around. Dizzard Wood is

Towards Sharnhole Point

Surveyor's Pillar

The concrete surveyor's pillar or trig point, at the Dizzard marks a height of 540 feet above sea level.

Stunted oak

open for public access but please take great care on the uneven ground and do not damage any wild plants.

(4) Continue along the coast path for about a hundred metres until you reach a waymark post pointing inland to Dizzard Farm. Walk across a field, past the end of a farm track and then continue down through some trees, across a stream and up until you reach a grassy lane which will take you past some farm buildings and out on to the road.

Waymark to Dizzard Farm

farm commands the steep valley beyond and which may once have been a tribal boundary. Go between the buildings and continue along the lane which leads you to the entrance to a Woodland Trust site and down through the woods. The footpath is enclosed by low banks and is one of a network of smugglers' trails used by packhorses to carry cargo inland from the coast.

6 At the bottom of the valley the path swings left to follow the stream on through Landy Wood. Cross the stream by a wooden bridge

5 Walk along the road to the right for a short section until you reach the farm road on the left to Trengayor. The name in Cornish means dwelling by the fortified place and the

The woods on the cliffs at Dizzard are more than 6,000 years old. As well as sessile oak trees, there are a few rare wild service trees whose fruits were once used to make a strong alcoholic liqueur.

and walk past the cottage into the access drive, a little way along climb the ladder stile and cross a wildflower meadow in front of the house. There is another ladder stile after which continue thorough the woods with the stream

on your left. Cross using the bridge just before another cottage and look out for a footpath signpost pointing straight along the valley to Millook (a favourite landing beach for smugglers) or left uphill to Cancleave; take the uphill path.

7 Up through the trees and then out into a field. The way crosses a field towards a cattle shed and a stile out on to the road. The car park is just a few yards to the left.

Wildflower meadow

6 Week St Mary and Penhallam

A shepherd girl who became Lady Mayoress of London, a fugitive hare and a rediscovered manor house.

The Anglo-Saxons established a market at Week St Mary and its long history is reflected in its stories and characters. This circular walk provides glimpses of this rich past including the first grammar school in England, strange carvings on the church tower and a tour through farms and woodland. Towards the end there is a steep section along a road.

Level: ♥ ♥
Length: 2.5 miles
Terrain: Fields and woodland with one steep road section
Parking: In Week St Mary square
Start Ref: SX 237976
Explorer Map 111

Church tower carvings

The College

① The square in front of the village shop and the church provides car parking. Go past the shop and walk left along the road until you come to a high castellated wall on your right. This is Week St Mary College which was founded in 1506 as a grammar school by Dame Thomasine Percival of London. As a child, she looked after the village sheep and geese. Hers was a true rags to riches story; a travelling merchant noticed her and took her to London. Thomasine married three times, her last husband being the Lord Mayor of London. In her will, Thomasine left money to found a school in her native village.

A market was held every week at Week St Mary for over 800 years and only closed within living memory.

② From the College, carry on for a few yards until you come to the Lower Square, go left into the churchyard. St Mary's church is a fine 14th and 15th century structure. The tower is a particular feature with its bands of carved stone; on the west side above the door is a worn carving of a hare and hounds. A local story tells how a hare being chased by hounds ran into the sanctuary of the churchyard but foolishly tried to make good its escape by scampering out over the roofs of the adjoining cottages, only to be caught and killed by the pack who had circled around.

3 Leave the churchyard along the pathway into the village square then turn right up the street and then right again. Pass the village hall on the left and at the bend in the road go through the farm gate which is straight ahead. Follow the drive downhill until you reach the buildings of Ashbury Farm. Go through the

Site of Bury Court

farmyard to the far gate where you bear left and through another gate into a field. Head downhill into woodland. You will find a way down through the trees until you come to a gate and stile leading to an old stone bridge over a little stream. Go through an area of damp woodland and then up on to a farm track where you turn right until you find a stile on the right.

4 The path leads into the site of Bury Court which is under the care of English Heritage; it is one of the few moated manor houses in Cornwall. Bury Court was forgotten for several hundred years and only revealed in 1967 when the area was being prepared for forestry planting. Excavations have uncovered a complex of buildings including a hall, bake house and tiny chapel; 800 years ago it was the summer home of one of the great Norman landholding families. Bury Court (or Penhallam as it was called in the Domesday Book) is a magical place.

5 Leave the site along the track provided by English Heritage. The ways now runs through forestry plantings; on the crown of the hill to the right, is an Iron Age fort or 'bury'

which gave its name to Bury Court and Ashbury Farm. Continue along the forest track until you reach the little car park and the road. The way back to Week St Mary is along the road to the right; this is narrow and uphill in places so take care.

6 After climbing the hill and passing a cottage on the right you will come to a junction in the road with a right hand sign for Week St Mary. After a few yards a footpath sign on the left directs you to the village. Go through the gate and keep close to the right hand hedge, at the bottom of this field you cross over a stile into a boggy patch. After this go up into the field and make your way straight up the hill with the tower of the church ahead. At the top there is a stile into

The Anglo-Saxon name for the village was Wyke which suggests that it was a centre for selling milk and cheese; St Mary was added later to distinguish it from other 'Wyke' places.

another small enclosure next to the churchyard. The humps and bumps in the grass here mark the site of a small Norman motte and bailey castle. From here you return to the churchyard and out to the village square.

Ashbury Iron Age fort

A short walk to a chieftain's camp, a giant's grave and a Domesday manor.

he Iron Age hill fort at Warbstow is one of the largest in the South West. It commands the surrounding countryside across to Dartmoor, the North Cornwall coast and beyond. Local traditions say that a giant, or even King Arthur, is buried here.

Level:
Length: 1.5 miles
Terrain: Fields and lanes
Parking: At entrance to Warbstow Bury
Start Ref: SX 203906
Explorer Map 111

Warbstow Bury
Treswen
Warbstow Cross
Tredarrup
Downinney
Tredarrup Cross

Old barn at Churchtown

Warbstow and Downinney

Warbstow Bury is a multi-vallate hillfort meaning
it has two or more lines of ramparts.

On Warbstow Bury in early Spring

Start. There is a car park at the entrance to Warbstow Bury and it is only a few steps to reach the 2500 year old hill fort. There are two ramparts with deep ditches between them and an entrance way into the central enclosure. A walk around the ramparts shows how the camp dominated the surrounding countryside. The scale of the defences and the resources needed to build them, suggest that this stronghold was the power base of an important chief.

In the central flat enclosure is a grassy mound. Historians are undecided about its origins or purpose; some claim it was a medieval rabbit warren, others that it is a Neolithic long barrow or something used during the performance of Cornish miracle plays. However, local legends are in no doubt that this is a grave. One story tells how a giant was buried here after a battle with a neighbour, another claims that King Arthur himself lies sleeping under the ground. Thankfully there has never been a serious attempt to excavate the mound because the legend tells that if it is ever disturbed a storm to end all storms will devastate the land.

Ancient building at Churchtown

3 From the Bury return to the car park and then go straight across the road and through the gate into a green lane. Follow this downhill until you reach the road and turn right. This is the Churchtown, a Cornish description for the farm and cottages situated close to a church but some distance from the main settlement. Make your way up towards the church and note the straggle of old buildings alongside the road. Many of these no longer have a modern use and are falling into decay but features such as stone windows and lintels, show that once they had a higher status.

4 Continue past the farm cottage and into the churchyard. Built on a mound, the surrounding roughly

Cornish stile at St Warburga's

Medieval windows at Churchtown

circular bank marks it as being of Celtic Christian origins. However the little 15th century church is dedicated to St Warburga and has been so since at least 1201. This daughter of a 7th century King of Mercia, has her shrine in far off Chester, so why her dedication here on a clearly Celtic site? Perhaps the Saxon settlers who took over the area from the native Cornish, wanted to demonstrate their authority so they ousted the local saint and named the church after one of their own.

(5) Leave the churchyard over a "cornish stile" in the hedge above the church, turn right along the farm lane and where it enters the fields, turn through the left hand gate. The views to the left are across to Dartmoor; follow the right hand hedge and cross over by the wooden stile about three-quarters along. After the stile, follow the hedge, now on your left, until you reach another stile. Climb over here carefully as it leads directly on to a rather steep bank down on to the narrow road.

Lane near Downinney

Warbstow and Downinney

6 Turn left down hill between high banks until you come to a junction where you follow the left hand sign to Downinney. This hamlet of a farm and a few cottages surrounds a village green or common. Now a quiet backwater, it was recorded in the Domesday Book as the manor of Donecheniv and home to 20 smallholders, 10 villagers and 20 slaves. In one corner of the Common there is a small enclosure which may once have been an animal pound.

Warbstow Bury is 790 feet above sea level and has extensive views in all directions except from the south-west and is built on the slope of the hill rather than right on the very top.

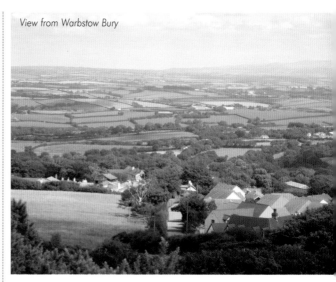

View from Warbstow Bury

7 Continue along the road which runs through the Common. After a short while, you will find a left hand junction which leads back to the church but continue past this and down into Warbstow Cross. Here is the main village, turn left and follow the road uphill until you reach the Bury car park.

8 Egloskerry Circular

A knight with a bad cold, a devil's door and ancient rights.

The village sits astride the old road from Launceston to Padstow and takes its name from one of the 24 children of the Welsh King Brychan all of whom brought Christianity to the West Country. This is a country walk through an ancient estate and provides glimpses of some striking 16th century buildings and ornamental gardens.

Level:
Length: 4.0 miles
Terrain: Fields and lanes.
Parking: In the village near the parish hall
Start Ref: SX 272866
Explorer Map 111

Penheale
Barton

■ Penheale Manor

River Ottery

■Trebeath
Farm

Beepark
Copse

Dismantled
Railway

Egloskerry ●

Dovecote at Penheale

47

Egloskerry village scene

There is parking along the roads in the village also next to the Parish Hall in Station Road. Make your way to the church of St Keri and St Petroc. The interior has suffered from the Victorian zeal for over-restoration, but it does have some special features. Above the door is a tympanum showing the Pascal Lamb and Flag while, tucked into a niche in the wall, there is a recumbent knight.

This unfortunate fellow seems either to have had a bad cold or perhaps was a heavy drinker, as his nose is quite red. In fact his affliction is the result of poor restoration works in the 19th century but it gives him a certain distinction! Before leaving the church, go around the outside to see the north doorway where a carving above the door shows a dragon or serpent. This represents the Devil who is supposed

The church at Egloskerry was one of ten chapels administered by Launceston Priory which now lies in ruins close to the River Kensey at nearby Newport.

to have been driven out of the church through this door when a child was baptised or a good man entered!

Red-nosed knight

Devil's doorway

2 From the church follow the public footpath next to the churchyard wall. This leads into the village playing field where you turn left along the hedge to a stile in the far corner, cross over and continue alongside the left hand hedge to the bottom of the field. Ahead you will see a gate and to the left a direction signpost; take the left fork and walk along the bottom of the field.

3 Continue with field hedge now on your right, ignore the first gate on the right and continue for a little further until you see a stile leading into some woodland and with a timber walkway. Using the walkway to cross a boggy area under the trees, go straight ahead and up into the next field. With the hedge on your left, walk up this gently sloping field until you see a gateway in the hedge. The pathway goes through this and then continues on with the hedge now on the right, until you reach a kissing gate in the top corner and so on to a farm lane.

4 Turn left here; the lane soon brings you on to the main drive to Penheale Manor. Follow the tree-lined drive to the right until you reach a fork where you branch right. Within a few yards you will see a splendid dovecote next to an archway into a yard. Turn right along the end

Egloskerry once had its own railway station and goods yard but the line was closed on 3 October 1966.

of the building and then follow the path which curves around the front of the building. The estate buildings are old but were remodelled in the last century by Sir Edward Lutyens and around the same time, the gardens were designed by Gertrude Jekyll.

Penheale Manor

(5) Across the lawns is the gatehouse to Penheale Manor. Unfortunately, this and its ornamental gardens are not open to the public. There has been a manor here since Norman times when it was held by King William. It has changed

hands several times since then but has always been in private ownership. However The lords of the manor have not always had everything their way. In 1889 an attempt was made to deprive the villagers of their ancient right to take turf and wood from parts of the estate and so they took their case to the High Court – and won.

(6) You now have the option to return back along the drive to the lane near the kissing gate or to continue down along the track for another few hundred metres. If you continue, you will pass a rather splendid pump house, then through some woodland to reach a fording place across the River Ottery. This little river was once of great significance. It divided an area of early Anglo-Saxon

settlement from the Celts and remained the boundary between Devon and Cornwall until 1966. The ford has probably existed since the first settlements were established and Penheale Manor may have been built here to control the crossing. From the river, return back through the estate to the lane by the kissing gate (point 4).

7 Do not go through the kissing gate but instead, go straight ahead along the track and through several gates. Pass Beepark Copse on the right and walk along the track through three more fields until you reach Coombekeale Farm. Turn right past the front of the house along the entrance drive. Where it curves left, turn down the muddy track on the right, across a shallow stream and follow the right

Ford over the Ottery

hand field hedge until, just before reaching a small copse, you turn right through a gateway. Continue with the hedge on your left, through another gate to the brow of the rise where the hedge turns away to the right and where there is a way into the field on the left.

Walk diagonally across this field towards the bottom hedge where you will find a broken down bridge over the stream and a gate which you first saw on the way out at Point 2. From here retrace the walk to the village.

9 St Juliot and Minster

A true romance at Camelot, a lost monastery and across the River Jordan to Paradise.

The little church of St Juliot nestles on the side of the Valency Valley inland from Boscastle This walk goes from the church where Thomas Hardy met his wife Emma, along the river, through the woods to a holy well and on to the Old Village at Boscastle.

Level:
Length: 5 miles
Terrain: Fields and steep woods with one road section
Parking: By St Juliot church
Start Ref: SX 129912
Explorer Map 111

Penally House
B3263
7
Boscastle
6
Minster Wood
5
Minster church + 4
3
2
St Juliot church 1 +
River Valency
South West Coast Path

Down the Valley

There is parking outside St Juliot church. From here the route goes through the churchyard, over a stile and down the steps overlooking the valley. There are two ancient crosses in the graveyard and the little church is worthy of attention and especially the window inside which has been finely engraved in memory of Thomas Hardy's association with this place. He first came here in 1870 to draw up a restoration plan for the church and was at once attracted by Miss Emma Gifford, who lived in the rectory with her sister and brother-in-law. This was the beginning of a lifelong and complex enchantment which stayed with Hardy even after Emma's death more than 40 years later.

Left: Churchyard
Above: Thomas Hardy's window

Track at Newmill

(2) From the steps, turn right and then over the stile in the field hedge. Continue along the bottom of the next two fields, and then after you pass in front of a cottage, go through the gate and on to the woodland path. Follow this track past a ruined house and soon out on to the narrow roadway. Go straight across at Newmill and continue down the valley with the Valency River on your left. Not long after the last cottage at Newmill, you will come to a bench close to a footbridge over the river and a signpost to Minster Church.

(3) Cross the footbridge and follow the steep footpath winding through the trees of Peter's Wood; this a nature reserve and an important habitat for several species of bats and rare lichens. As you reach the brow of the hill, you leave the path and bear right towards the church which you can glimpse through the trees ahead. Minster church is dedicated to St Merthiana, a female saint of the 6th or 7th centuries and whose body is believed to be buried here.

In the 19th century a farm worker found an ancient Celtic golden necklace on a farm near St Juliot church but thought it was worthless brass and was persuaded to sell it for a few pence.

Minster Church

Minster Church

4   In the 12th century a small Benedictine priory was founded here on the site of the early Celtic church. The church and priory became the centre of a religious community where the shrine and holy well of the saint were important features. The monks at Minster owed their allegiance to Angers in France and this connection caused problems during the many periods when England was at war with France. Within 300 years the monastery was abandoned, although the church, as the mother church of Boscastle, remained in use. The building was remodelled in the 15th and 19th centuries and little remains of the original structure. A curious carving of a pair of shears built into the exterior of the tower may have been part of the priory. Below the

Carving on tower

The valleys here were the catchment for the rain which caused the devastating floods in August 2004 which swept cars away and damaged many buildings in Boscastle.

church, the holy well of St Merthiana still runs with clear water.

(5) Leave the churchyard by the stile or gate and turn right along the narrow road. At the first junction continue right, past the entrance to Home Farm downhill until at a bend you will see a stile and footpath sign on the right pointing to Old Boscastle Village; climb the stile and walk diagonally across the field to the far left corner. Ignore the National Trust footpath sign pointing right to Minster Wood and instead take the path which runs alongside the river. This will take you in front of a cottage where you cross over the river on to

the drive which will lead you out to the road at Fore Street in the old part of Boscastle. The river you have crossed is the Jordan and part of the village near here is called Paradise.

St Merthiana's holy well

6 As ever, there is no time for Paradise so turn right downhill. Along the way you will pass ancient cottages, the village school and chapel. Towards the bottom of the hill you will see the Wellington Hotel.

7 The centre of Boscastle has been rebuilt following devastating floods in the summer of 2004 and the picturesque harbour area is a favourite tourist destination. Turn right over the bridge and make your way through the car park to join the footpath which runs close to the bank of the River Valency. A beautiful walk at any time of the year.

View from Old Village path

8 Continue along the river path until you come to the footbridge across to Peter's Wood and Minster church; from here retrace your footsteps to St Juliot church. This was a walk familiar to Thomas Hardy and his Emma and is at the heart of the land he called Lyonnesse.

10 Rocky Valley

The most dramatic and most mysterious valley in Cornwall where you can ask for a wish, see an ancient good luck symbol and walk along a haunted river.

Starting with a walk along the coast, this route then turns inland to follow a stream up Rocky Valley with its dramatic waterfalls, ruined mill and ancient rock carvings and a place of charms. Further inland there is the option to take a loop in the walk which will press further up river to visit a holy well and a rediscovered place of worship.

Level: 🥾 🥾 🥾
Length: 4.5 miles
Terrain: Cliffs and woodland with some uneven and steep sections.
Parking: By the telephone kiosk and public conveniences at Bosinney Cove.
Start Ref: SX 067889
Explorer Map 111

Rocky Valley

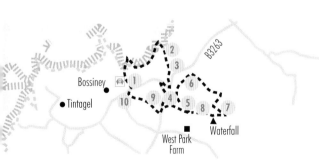

Path to Bossiney Haven

① Start at the lane to Bossiney Haven where there is parking near the telephone kiosk and radio mast. Go through the gate towards the coast and continue until you reach the coast path where you turn right towards Rocky Valley. Enjoy the fine views along the dramatic cliffs to Long Island; continue until you reach the steep steps down to Rocky Valley. Turn inland before the bridge over the river.

Until 1845 there was a silver mine on the cliffs near Rocky Valley.

② The path follows the river which has cut through the soft rocks of the Valley to create a gorge. If you stand on the high rocks just where the river joins the sea, you can feel why this is a place which has attracted poets, painters and songwriters. Continue inland to cross the river to the ruins of Trewethett Mill. The buildings have been abandoned for over 100 years but it was once a flourishing woollen mill.

Left: Where the river meets the sea
Above: Ruined mill

(3) Just behind the mill, two small labyrinth patterns have been carved into the rock face. Similar carved symbols in Europe are believed to be more than 2000 years old and labyrinth patterns are found in many ancient cultures. Expert opinion is divided over these two carvings; their excellent condition suggests they were carved in comparatively recent times. Whenever it was made, the labyrinth is an age old symbol of rebirth and renewal and it is in this spirit that many people are now leaving offerings and gifts here.

(4) Follow the path up stream. Over the bridge in front of Trevillett Mill cottages and then out on to the road. Taking great care, cross directly over and take the road up

For three hundred years, two Members of Parliament were elected by the voters of Bossiney and nearby Trevena, including Sir Frances Drake in 1584.

towards Halgabron; this is steep but fortunately not too long. At Halgabron you can either continue for a short way over fields to return to the car park (go to point 9) or take a loop down into a steep valley and up the other side to the holy well or church at Trethevy.

Labyrinth carving

(5) To reach the valley, take the footpath on the left over a stile and diagonally across to the corner of the field to reach an old wrought iron kissing gate into the woods. Follow the path down to the stream and cross by the footbridge. Here you will see a signpost which points right to St Nectan's Glen and left to Trethevy; turn left. The path soon reaches an access road which you follow uphill (past many sainted properties!) to reach Trethevy. Here you will find a holy well dedicated to St Piran and a tiny church also dedicated to the patron saint of Cornwall. First recorded in 1457,

the church was later used as farm shed but was restored to its proper use in the 1940s when the grave of a medieval priest was found near the entrance.

(6) Not only the holy well and its medieval church mark this as a special place. In one of the private gardens here there is a Roman milestone from about AD250 which was probably erected to mark the way to the royal settlement at nearby Tintagel. Take the track uphill next to the church (marked Unsuitable for Motors) and keep to this all the way until you reach the

Footpath signpost

entrance to The Hermitage perched on the side of the valley.

(7) Just below here the river plunges down through a hole in the rock, known as St Nectan's Kieve (Cornish for basin). Legends associated with the Kieve are that the saint's body and silver bell are buried under a great rock, that pilgrims came

here to bathe in the waters, and that the valley is haunted by the ghosts of two mysterious sisters who watch over the resting place of St. Nectan's treasure. To reach the Kieve you have to pay an entrance fee.

8 The public right of way goes past The Hermitage and down into the valley to the river. When you reach the footbridge which you crossed earlier and turned to reach Trethevy, recross and retrace your steps to Halgabron.

9 At the road, turn left and very soon you will find a footpath on the right which takes you across one field to a stile, straight across the next field and then diagonally over a third field down to a little wooded valley.

River near St Nectan's Kieve

Halgabron *means* carrion crow marsh *in the Cornish language.*

10 Cross the stream and make your way through a holiday park to reach a stile which leads on to the road at Bossiney. Cross over and turn right to reach the car park.